TAKE ACTION

SAVE LIFE ON EARTH

# SAVE OCEAN LIFE

Stephanie Feldstein

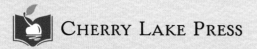

## CHERRY LAKE PRESS

Published in the United States of America by Cherry Lake Publishing Group
Ann Arbor, Michigan
www.cherrylakepublishing.com

Reading Adviser: Beth Walker Gambro, MS, Ed., Reading Consultant, Yorkville, IL
Book Designer: Felicia Macheske

Photo Credits: © Rich Carey/Shutterstock, cover; © Eric Isselee/Shutterstock, 5; © Luiz Felipe V. Puntel/ Shutterstock, 5; © Kletr/Shutterstock, 5, back cover; © SergeUWPhoto/Shutterstock, 9; Library of Congress, Howard Liberman, photographer. Workers at the Glenn L. Martin Bomber Plant. Baltimore, Maryland. , 1942.; LOC Control No: 2017767760, 11; © Richard Whitcombe/Shutterstock, 13; © orifec_a31/Shutterstock, © Rich Carey/ Shutterstock, 17; © Bilanol/Shutterstock, © Scott Lupro/Shutterstock, 21; © Rise St. James, 23; © Jewelzz/ Shutterstock, 25; © setthayos sansuwansri/Shutterstock, 26; © Marlon Lopez MMG1 Design/Shutterstock, 29; © bluehand/Shutterstock, back cover

Graphics Credits: © Lena Pronne/Shutterstock; © Pavel K/Shutterstock; © Panimoni/Shutterstock; © Hulinska Yevheniia/Shutterstock; © Vector Place/Shutterstock; © Hein Nouwens/Shutterstock; © Sugiwara/Shutterstock; © Nadiinko/Shutterstock; © Cube29/Shutterstock; © Nsit/Shutterstock

**Cherry Lake Press** is an imprint of Cherry Lake Publishing Group.

Library of Congress Cataloging-in-Publication Data has been filed and is available at catalog.loc.gov.

Cherry Lake Publishing Group would like to acknowledge the work of the Partnership for 21st Century Learning, a Network of Battelle for Kids. Please visit *http://www.battelleforkids.org/networks/p21* for more information.

Printed in the United States of America
Corporate Graphics

Note from publisher: Websites change regularly, and their future contents are outside of our control. Supervise children when conducting any recommended online searches for extended learning opportunities.

# Table of Contents

# INTRODUCTION

# Oceans and the Extinction Crisis

Floating plastic bags look like jellyfish in the ocean. Sea turtles think they are a tasty snack. Instead, they get a stomach full of plastic. When this happens, they can't eat their other food. Plastic waste kills ocean animals. It kills more than one million every year.

**Extinction** is when all of one kind of plant or animal dies. It affects wild plants and animals. An extinct plant or animal is gone forever. Scientists say we're in an extinction **crisis**. When wildlife goes extinct, it weakens **ecosystems**. Healthy ecosystems provide food, shelter, water, and clean air. Life on Earth needs all kinds of plants and animals.

More than 70 percent of our planet is covered by oceans. These huge bodies of water are filled with life. Ocean animals can be tiny. One of these animals is **zooplankton**. Zooplankton are small floating animals. They can be as small as one cell. Other ocean animals are huge. Blue whales are longer than three school buses! These different animals depend on each other. One animal going extinct can affect the entire ecosystem.

More than 80 percent of the oceans haven't been explored. There's a lot we don't know about them. But we do know they face many threats. **Climate change** harms ocean life. **Overfishing** and plastic **pollution** are harmful, too. These threats are caused by people.

We can stop the extinction crisis. People need to take action. Governments and businesses need to act, too. By working together, we can save our oceans.

# Why We Need
# HEALTHY OCEANS

The oceans sustain all life on Earth. Many land animals rely on oceans for food. Seafood also feeds people around the world. People use oceans for transportation and jobs. They are important in many cultural traditions.

People often think of trees making the oxygen we breathe. But plants, algae, and bacteria in the oceans also make oxygen. More than half of Earth's oxygen comes from the oceans.

The oceans shape the weather. The water gets warm from the Sun. This warm water creates storms. The ocean water moves in patterns

called currents. Currents carry warm and cold water across the oceans. They help keep Earth's temperatures stable.

Oceans absorb about 30 percent of the world's carbon dioxide. Too much carbon dioxide makes the water acidic. This makes it harder for many species to survive. Climate change is heating up ocean water too quickly. Warmer water makes weather less predictable. It also makes storms stronger. Climate change, overfishing, and pollution put the entire food chain at risk.

# CHAPTER ONE

# Troubled Waters

The oceans face many threats. Climate change causes **ocean acidification**. This changes the chemistry of the water. Acidic water affects ocean life in different ways. One example is that animals like oysters can't build shells. Animals with shells are important to the ecosystem. They provide food and shelter for others. When animals can't build shells, it hurts the whole ecosystem.

Fisheries catch nearly 100 million tons of fish for seafood each year. Almost 90 percent of these fish are overfished. Overfishing is when too many of one kind of fish has been caught. Overfishing can increase the fish's chances of going extinct.

Cutting back on eating seafood can help fish species recover from overfishing.

# TURNING POINT

Plastic was invented more than 100 years ago. But it wasn't used very much at first. That changed during World War II (1939–1945). Plastic was used for many different kinds of military gear. Production grew quickly. After the war, plastic factories began making products for homes. Soon plastic products were everywhere.

That meant plastic trash was everywhere, too. Rain and wind carry plastic into rivers and streams. Those waterways drain into the oceans. Scientists started to see plastic in the oceans in the 1960s. People worried about it hurting the environment. But factories kept making more plastic. The amount of plastic in the world kept growing. So did the amount of plastic pollution. We make twice as much plastic today as 20 years ago.

In the 1940s, plastic was used during World War II to make airplane parts. After the war, it was used to make many different products.

Most plastic isn't recycled. It stays in the environment for hundreds of years. Scientists are looking for ways to clean up plastic pollution. Making less plastic is the best way to stop the problem from getting worse.

The seafood industry uses huge nets and fishing lines. Millions of other animals are caught in this fishing gear. This is called **bycatch**. These animals are not sold. They're left to die in the oceans. Bycatch includes fish that aren't eaten as seafood. Birds are also bycatch. Marine mammals like whales, dolphins, and seals are caught, too. More than 650,000 marine mammals are killed as bycatch every year.

Fish can get tangled in plastic trash and drown. Sea turtles, birds, and even whales can get tangled, too. These animals also eat plastic every day. Blue whales are the largest animal on Earth. They can eat as much as 96 pounds (44 kilograms) of plastic in one day.

Nearly a million tons of fishing gear is left behind in the sea per year. It's lost or thrown away in the water. This gear is called "**ghost gear**." It makes up about 10 percent of ocean plastic. The seafood industry causes this pollution. You can choose to eat less fish and other seafood. Then you won't be supporting the industry's pollution.

The Sun and waves break down larger pieces of plastic over time. They become tiny pieces that stay in the environment. These tiny pieces are called **microplastics**. Microplastics are so small that they're easily eaten by animals. They fill up the animals so they can't eat real food. They also contain chemicals that make the animals sick.

◀ Whale sharks eat zooplankton, but they also end up eating microplastics that are also floating in the ocean.

# CHAPTER TWO

# Stop Plastic Pollution

Ocean animals will keep eating plastic as long as we keep throwing it away. Recycling isn't enough. Only 9 percent of all the plastic ever made has been recycled. The rest is in landfills and the oceans. We need to use less plastic.

Plastic is all around us. Many kinds of plastic we use once and throw away. Reusable products can replace plastic. Reusable products are made to be used more than once. They're made from materials like metal, glass, or cloth. They aren't as harmful to wildlife.

Switching to reusable products can help prevent ocean animals from eating plastic or getting tangled in plastic waste.

Most plastic comes from fossil fuels. **Oil refineries** separate oil into different parts. Some parts are used to make fuel. Others make plastic. Imagine one-fourth of a water bottle filled with oil. That's how much oil is used to make the bottle.

These industries are often in Black communities. The communities experience too much pollution. Plastic creates pollution every step of the way. It stops people from living safe, healthy lives. This makes plastic an **environmental justice** problem.

Eight out of ten pieces of litter found on the beach are plastic. Forty-four percent of these pieces come from places we eat. There are lots of plastic cups and take-out containers. There are also plastic straws and cutlery. This litter can be eaten by animals on the beach. The waves can sweep it into the oceans. Then it harms fish and other animals.

Restaurants need to use less plastic. That will make it easier for customers to use less. Use your own silverware from home when you get take-out meals. Don't use plastic forks, knives, and spoons. Ask servers in restaurants not to give you a straw. Bring your own containers for leftover food. Ask the places where you eat to replace plastic with reusable products. They can help save ocean life.

A lot of plastic waste comes from packaging. Toys, clothes, electronics, and other products are wrapped in plastic. Shipping boxes are usually packed full of plastic. Most of that plastic can't be reused or recycled. Write a letter to companies asking them to cut out plastic packaging.

Some cities and states ban plastic shopping bags. This means businesses aren't allowed to give them out. People bring their own cloth bags to stores instead. That's fewer plastic bags that could end up in the oceans. Ask your city council to pass a plastic bag ban. Bring your own reusable bags to the store. You can set an example even if plastic bags are allowed.

Many animals in the ocean mistake plastic bags ▶ for jellyfish when they are hunting for food.

# CONSERVATION CHAMPION

Sharon Lavigne lives in St. James Parish in Louisiana. St. James is a mostly Black community. It's in an area known as "Cancer Alley." It has hundreds of factories, oil refineries, and pipelines. They create a lot of pollution. It causes cancer in many of the people who live there.

Lavigne is a retired special education teacher. Now she works to fight the industries hurting her community. She started a group called RISE St. James. They wanted to stop a new plastic plant from being built.

The first meeting was in Lavigne's living room. There were only a few volunteers. They went door-to-door to talk to neighbors. They held meetings to educate others. They wrote to newspapers to argue against the plant. They talked to local council members. Environmental groups across the country joined their fight.

In 2019, Lavigne's group won a major victory. The plastic plant would not be built. Less new plastic waste would end up in the oceans.

Lavigne continues to fight for her community. Thanks to her work, people know more about Cancer Alley. She also showed that we can stop new plastic from being made. This is important to **conservation**. Conservation is action to protect wildlife and nature. Fewer plastic plants will help save ocean life.

# CHAPTER THREE

# Zero Waste Communities

Some people try to produce as little trash as possible. This movement is called **zero waste**. It helps make their impact on the planet smaller. Zero waste is more than just not throwing things away. It also means stopping waste from ever being made. That includes buying only what you need.

It can be very hard to cut back on waste on our own. We often don't have many choices in stores. Grocery stores may only offer food like bread wrapped in plastic. Restaurants may only have plastic cups. Reusable choices can be harder to find.

Your choices help protect ocean life. But none of us can do this alone. We need plastic-free choices everywhere we go. Cities and businesses need to help.

Reducing plastic in the ocean and on beaches can help these baby sea turtles survive.

Most plastic has a recycling symbol on it. It also often has writing telling you to recycle it. But most plastic can't be recycled. There are too many different kinds. They can't be easily sorted and melted. Only 5 percent of plastic in the United States is recycled.

Zero-waste communities are popping up around the world. The best ones go beyond recycling. They make it easy not to create waste in the first place.

Buying things secondhand is better for the planet. They don't come with wasteful packaging. They don't use the fossil fuels, land, and water needed to make new things. They don't add to factory pollution.

The small town of Kamikatsu, Japan, has a "swap shop." People can leave things they don't need. Others can come to the shop and pick them up for free. The town of Flanders in Belgium gives money to secondhand shops. These towns also help people keep trash out of landfills.

Zero-waste stores don't use plastic packaging. They help shoppers avoid plastic waste. They use glass jars, paper bags, and other reusable containers. Some stores allow you to bring your own containers to refill. These stores show that many things have more packaging than they need. Getting rid of wasteful plastic can help protect ocean life.

# SPEAK UP FOR OCEAN LIFE

Have you ever opened a game to find each part in its own plastic sleeve? Or maybe you received a box mostly filled with plastic. All that extra plastic packaging usually heads straight to the trash. Companies need to stop using wasteful plastic. Then there will be less in the environment.

Think about the companies that make your favorite video games, toys, or snacks. Look at their packaging. See if you can spot plastic that doesn't need to be there. Go to the company's website. Look for their contact or customer service information. It's often at the bottom of the site. Or it may be under a "contact us" menu. Find a mailing address, email address, or online form where you can send them a message.

Do you wish companies would use less plastic? You can write to ask them to stop.

**Your message should have four key parts:**

1. **Tell them why you love their products. This lets them know you're really a customer. It makes your message feel more personal.**
2. **Ask them to help stop plastic pollution. Tell them to stop using plastic packaging. Let them know if you have an idea of where they can start.**
3. **Tell them why this is important. Use the facts you learned in this book.**
4. **Ask them to tell you what steps they'll take to get rid of plastic waste.**

**It's a good idea to have a friend or family member read your letter. They can help make sure it's clear. They can also check for typos before you send it to the company.**

# ACTIVITY

# CREATE YOUR OWN REUSE COMMUNITY

You don't have to live by the coast to help save ocean life. Using less plastic keeps it out of the oceans. Your choices set an example for others. People will see how to use less plastic. They'll see how to **reuse** instead.

Here's how you can help create a reuse community:

1 Ask your town to become a zero-waste community. Write to your local council members. Tell them to take action to reduce waste. They can ban single-use plastic. They can support reuse and secondhand businesses. They can join zero-waste cities around the world.

2 Ask large public places to help. Sports stadiums and theaters can get involved. They can ban plastic straws. They can stop selling plastic bottles of water. They can install water stations. People can use these stations to refill their own bottles.

3 Ask your school to stop using plastic in the cafeteria. Talk to your teacher about how your class can speak up. You can work together to write letters.

4 Make your own reuse kit. It should have containers for food leftovers. Add silverware so you don't have to use plastic forks and spoons. Keep the kit in your backpack or your family's car. That way, you'll have reusable items wherever you go. Carry a water bottle you can refill. Once other people see you doing it, they'll get inspired to do it, too.

## LEARN MORE

Hyde, Natalie. *Preventing Ocean Pollution*. New York, NY: Crabtree Publishing Co., 2021.

Knutson, Julie. *Do the Work! Climate Action, Life Below Water, and Life on Land*. Ann Arbor, MI: Cherry Lake Publishing, 2022.

Salt, Rachel. *The Plastic Problem*. Richmond Hill, ON: Firefly Books, 2019.

## GLOSSARY

**bycatch** (BY-kach) animals accidentally caught and killed by fishing gear

**climate change** (KLY-muht CHAYNJ) changes in weather, temperatures, and other natural conditions over time

**conservation** (kahn-suhr-VAY-shuhn) action to protect wildlife and nature

**crisis** (KRY-suhss) a very difficult time or emergency

**ecosystems** (EE-koh-sih-stuhmz) places where plants, animals, and the environment rely on each other

**environmental justice** (in-vye-ruh-MEN-tuhl JUH-stuhs) the right of all people to live in a safe, healthy environment

**extinction** (ik-STINK-shuhn) when all of one kind of plant or animal dies

**ghost gear** (GOHST GIHR) fishing gear that is lost or thrown away in the oceans

**microplastics** (my-kroh-PLAH-stiks) tiny pieces of plastic broken down by the Sun and waves

**ocean acidification** (OH-shuhn uh-sih-duh-fuh-KAY-shuhn) when an ocean's chemistry changes from too much carbon dioxide

**oil refineries** (OYL rih-FYE-nuh-reez) industrial plants that separate oil into different products such as fuel and plastic

**overfishing** (oh-vuhr-FIH-shing) catching too many of one kind of fish

**pollution** (puh-LOO-shuhn) harmful materials released into the environment

**reuse** (ree-YOOZ) to use packaging or products many times instead of throwing them away

**zero waste** (ZIHR-oh WAYST) the movement to stop creating trash by changing the way things are made, bought, used, and thrown away

## INDEX